How dreams are built

Creating Your Own Route to Happiness

By

Israel Daniel

Disclaimer

By Israel Daniel, copyright © 2024. All rights reserved. This ebook's content is intended solely for informative and educational purposes. It is not meant to serve as a replacement for expert financial guidance. This ebook's publishers and writers are not financial counselors; thus, the information inside should not be interpreted as individual financial advice. Before making any financial decisions or putting any of the methods covered in this ebook into practice, readers are strongly advised to speak with licensed financial advisors. Any harm or injury arising from reliance on the information supplied herein is disclaimed by the writers and publishers.

Table of contents

Introduction
Chapter 1: Overview: Exposing the Dreams Blueprint
Chapter 2: Dream Interpretation: Getting Around the Inside World
Chapter 3: Establishing the Basis: Constructing the Foundational Elements of Goals
Chapter 4: Putting the Pieces Together: Creating the Road to Success
Chapter 5: Fostering Innovation: Unlocking the Potential of Imagination
Chapter 6: Creating Your Route: Managing the Path to Success
Chapter 7: The Value of Persistence: Maintaining Motion Despite Obstacles
Chapter 8: Networking and Cooperation: Building Connections for Success
Chapter 9: Managing Uncertainty and Taking Risks to Reach Your Goals
Chapter 10: Maintaining the Flames: Maintaining Momentum
Chapter 11: Realizing Your Dreams: An Introspective and Generous Path
Conclusion: Accepting the Journey

Introduction

In the world of human endeavor, dreams are the beacons of light that point us in the direction of a purposeful and prosperous future. The process of realizing our desires, from the lowest starting points to the highest goals, is a monument to the human spirit's tenacity and the limitless potential that everyone of us possesses.

In "How Dreams Are Built," we set out on an arduous voyage of inquiry and revelation, exploring the complex web of aspiration, tenacity, and inventiveness that molds our quest for fulfillment. We reveal the keys to turning dreams into reality and opening the doors to a meaningful and significant existence via the prism of personal experiences, perceptive observations, and useful tactics.

We come across barriers and difficulties that try our will and drive us to the limits of our capabilities as we make our way through the ups and downs of the human experience. However, it is during these times of hardship that we find our actual strength and resilience, as we learn to use our willpower and tenacity to go beyond any barriers that stand in our way.

However, pursuing our ambitions is a collaborative process. We have a network of friends, allies, and mentors who help us along the journey by providing direction, inspiration, and encouragement. Their guidance and encouragement provide a solid base for our dreams, giving us the bravery and fortitude to follow our goals with steadfast dedication and fervor.

In "How Dreams Are Built," we unearth the fundamental components that propel us on our path to fulfillment, from the value of vision and clarity to the strength of teamwork and perseverance. We gain the ability to successfully negotiate the complexity of risk and uncertainty, rising to the challenges that lay ahead with bravery and tenacity.

Let's keep in mind that pursuing our aspirations is a journey of self-discovery and progress rather than just a destination as we set out on this adventure together. Knowing that the journey itself is the best reward, we get closer to realizing our dreams with every step we take. Come along with me as we set off on this exciting journey to realizing our aspirations and opening up the limitless potential that each of us possesses. Let's embrace the difficulties, rejoice in the successes, and dare to dream of a time when there will be no shortage of passion, purpose, and fulfillment.

Chapter 1: Overview: Exposing the Dreams Blueprint

Dreams are the threads that bring our goals to life in the vast tapestry of human existence. They are the unseen designers of our destiny, the hints of hope that fan the spark of our ambition. However, what exactly are dreams? Do they have any real-world relevance, or are they just products of our imagination?

Determining Dreams

In the first chapter of our adventure, we set out to solve the mysteries of dreams. We go deeply into the essence of these mysterious beings, revealing their complex nature and the wide range of shapes they can take. We try to distill the essence of dreaming, from the transient visions of the night to the unwavering convictions of the soul.

By examining the subject of dreams through the prisms of psychology, philosophy, and introspection, we want to reveal the concepts hidden beneath layers of ambiguity. We look at how dreams influence our identities, motivate our goals, and help us realize our full potential. By utilizing the knowledge of professors and sages, we try to distill the meaning of dreams into a clear understanding potion.

The Vision's Power

We encounter the transformational power of vision

as we delve deeper into the core of our investigation. Dreams come to life as attainable objectives and desires when viewed through the prism of vision. However, vision is a guiding light that lights the way ahead and gives our journey direction and purpose; it is more than just a map.

We attest to the significant influence that vision can have on our lives through motivational tales and actual cases. We witness how the force of vision has impacted history and changed the world around us, from the lofty accomplishments of visionary leaders to the modest goals of common people. However, vision is a deliberate decision that we make every day rather than just the result of external events. It is the readiness to look past the limitations of the here and now and picture a world full of opportunities. We are urged to develop the bravery to dream big and the clarity to pursue our goals with unflinching determination as we set out on our own search for vision. Dreams are turned into reality, and the commonplace becomes remarkable in the furnace of vision. Here, in the infinite reaches of our imagination, is where we find the real power of dreams—the ability to mold our fate and permanently alter our lives.

Closing Thoughts: Venturing Into the Dream World

We are left feeling incredibly in awe of and amazed by the limitless potential that each of us possesses as we bring our investigation to a close. We have discovered the complex tapestry of dreams that embodies the core of our humanity, reaching from the depths of our subconscious to the zenith of our ambitions. Equipped with recently acquired understanding and motivation, we find ourselves on the cusp of opportunity, prepared to set off on a path of self-exploration and metamorphosis. We go out into the vastness of the unknown, eager to forge our own path and forge our own destiny among the always-changing currents of life, with the strength of our vision serving as our compass and the illuminating light of our dreams serving as our north star.

Let us keep in mind the lessons we have learned and the truths we have discovered along the way as we navigate these unexplored waters. Because when we follow our aspirations, we not only get what we truly want, but we also discover that we are capable of being the masterminds behind our own success.

So, my dear reader, I cordially welcome you to accompany me on this amazing voyage into the dream world—a voyage of exploration, revelation, and metamorphosis unmatched by any other. Because it is through pursuing our ambitions that we find the true meaning of humanity and unlock the limitless potential that everyone of us possesses.

Chapter 2: Dream Interpretation: Getting Around the Inside World

Dreams navigate the territory of our subconscious and act as a map and compass in the maze that is the human psyche. We must first solve the riddles surrounding our dreams, examining their varied manifestations and figuring out their underlying significance, before we can set off on this path of self-discovery.

Dream Types

There are countless patterns and motifs in the enormous fabric of dreams, and each one has its own meaning and symbolism. In this chapter, we set out to sort and organize the wide range of dreams that occupy our nighttime environments. We examine the range of human experience as mirrored in our subconscious rambles, from the fanciful worlds of dreams to the eerie specters of nightmares.

We explore the area of lucid dreaming, in which the distinction between dreaming and waking is blurred and the dreamer takes on the role of creator of their own reality. We study the fundamental principles governing dream production and content using the prisms of psychology and neuroscience. We explore the depths of our subconscious in quest of unspoken truths and unsolved issues, and we unveil the mysterious nature of recurrent dreams. However, dreams are dynamic, ever-evolving tapestries that intertwine the strands of our past, present, and future; they are not only passive projections of our deepest wants and thoughts. We examine the various ways that dreams influence and enlighten our lives, from symbolic dreams that use metaphor and allegory to prophetic dreams that reveal the course of fate.

Opening Up Your Dreams

Every desire starts with an aspirational kernel, a potential seed just waiting to be tended to and developed. This chapter takes us inward as we go on a quest of self-discovery to explore the hidden dimensions of our goals.

We explore the depths of our desires and motivations by delving deeply into the corners of our awareness, based on the ideas of introspection and reflection.

We uncover the hidden gems of our souls through facilitated activities and thought-provoking questions, shedding light on the road to fulfillment and self-realization.

However, ambitions are more than just fanciful thoughts or idle dreams; they are the impetus behind our greatest accomplishments and the engines of our own development. Our fantasies, no matter how grandiose or modest, are the way to releasing our actual selves and fulfilling our most ardent desires.

We face the worries and concerns that frequently prevent us from following our dreams as we make our way through the terrain of our desires.

We learn to accept the inherent dangers and uncertainties that come with pursuing our goals when we face the terrifying threat of rejection and failure. But through the difficulties and roadblocks we confront, we learn the strength of resiliency and willpower—the steadfast resolve to meet hardship head-on and come out stronger and more resilient than before.

We carve a way through the furnace of hardship, led by the light of our goals and the unwavering belief that our objectives are achievable. We find the real meaning of our goals—the hopes and dreams that make us who we are and help us reach our full potential—in the furnace of self-discovery. We set out on a path of transformation with a renewed sense of purpose and clarity, driven by the unyielding conviction that our aspirations are not just fantasies but rather the blueprints for our future.

In conclusion, getting started on the road to self-discovery

We are filled with a deep sense of amazement and wonder at the limitless potential that each of us possesses as we come to the end of our investigation into dreams and ambitions. We have set off on a unique voyage of self-discovery that has revealed the way to fulfillment and self-realization, taking us from the depths of our subconscious to the pinnacles of our ambitions. Equipped with recently acquired awareness and comprehension, we are prepared to welcome the transforming potential of our goals and desires as we stand on the cusp of opportunity. We ventured into the unknown with courage as our compass and determination as our guide, sure that we could negotiate the curves and turns of the road ahead.

And even though the journey may be drawn out and difficult, we find comfort in the understanding that we are not alone in our search for meaning and purpose; our dreams serve as the threads that bind us together. Because it is through pursuing our ambitions that we find the true meaning of humanity and unlock the limitless potential that everyone of us possesses.

Chapter 3: Establishing the Basis: Constructing the Foundational Elements of Goals

Every great accomplishment in the enormous field of human endeavor starts with a strong foundation, a bedrock of morals and values that provide direction through life's turbulent waves. We go on an introspective and self-discovery trip in this section, which paves the way for us to pursue our aspirations.

Finding your core beliefs

Every person has a distinct set of values at their core— fundamental ideas and concepts that help define who we are and guide our decisions. In this chapter, we explore the depths of our consciousness, revealing the foundation that supports our goals. We uncover the underlying truths that speak to us by removing the layers of training and society expectations through introspective activities and guided meditations. We probe the depths of our souls in pursuit of clarity and understanding as we face the existential dilemmas that sit at the crossroads of our values and desires.

Finding our values, however, is a process of self-discovery that involves lining up our behaviors with our highest goals and convictions. It's more than just an academic exercise. We learn to negotiate the intricacies of the human experience with grace and humility as we make our way through the maze-like interior environment, confronting the tensions and contradictions that emerge when our ideals and desires collide.

Through the trial by fire of self-discovery, we uncover the tenets that will act as our road map going forward. Our values are the moral compass that guides us towards our true north, which is the accomplishment of our deepest wants and the fulfillment of our highest aspirations, whether they take the shape of resilience, compassion, or honesty.

How to Write a Mission Statement

We begin the process of creating a mission statement, a succinct statement of purpose that describes our future vision and the actions we plan to take to realize it, using our values as a guide. In this chapter, we go on a voyage of self-examination and introspection, reducing the core of our goals to a concise and doable success plan.

We clarify our objectives and aims through a series of guided exercises and introspective prompts, pinpointing the significant turning points that will indicate our progress along the road. We face the anxieties and worries that frequently prevent us from going for our goals, and we learn to accept the difficulties and unknowns that come with aiming for the stars. Creating a mission statement, however, is a process of self-discovery—a way to bring our behaviors into alignment with our core beliefs and values. It's more than just a useful exercise. We address the existential issues that sit at the nexus of our goals and our purpose as we formulate our future vision, developing the clarity and self-assurance necessary to successfully negotiate the intricacies of the human experience.

Through the process of self-examination, we reduce the core of our goals to a concise and feasible mission statement—a statement of intent that functions as a road map for our accomplishments. Our mission statement, whether it is one sentence or a multi-sentence manifesto, is the lighthouse that points the way forward and gives our journey direction, clarity, and purpose.

In conclusion, establishing the foundation for success

We have gained a strong sense of purpose and clarity as we come to the end of our investigation into laying the groundwork for success. This will serve as our road map for the future. We have established a strong foundation of purpose and conviction that will stand the test of time, spanning from the lowest points of our beliefs to the highest points of our aspirations. Equipped with lucidity and resolve, we are positioned on the cusp of opportunity, prepared to set off on an unparalleled voyage of introspection and metamorphosis. We ventured into the unknown, sure that we could find our way around the curves in the road ahead, using our mission statement as a road map and our values as a guide. We find comfort in knowing that we are not alone in our search for meaning and purpose, even though the journey may be long and full of obstacles. Our values and goals serve as the threads that link us together. Because it is through pursuing our ambitions that we find the true meaning of humanity and unlock the limitless potential that everyone of us possesses.

Chapter 4: Putting the Pieces Together: Creating the Road to Success

Success in chasing our aspirations is a journey rather than a destination, one that is shaped by the small actions we take and the challenges we face along the way. In this section, we examine the fundamental building blocks that lead to success, such as goal-setting and overcoming unforeseen obstacles.

Techniques for Setting Goals

Every successful project starts with a distinct and compelling objective, which is the end point we pursue with unshakable focus and drive. This chapter delves into the art and science of goal-setting, examining methods and approaches that assist us in expressing our desires and laying out a plan to achieve them.

We define our goals and desires and break them down into doable tasks and benchmarks through a series of facilitated exercises and introspective prompts. We study the SMART (specific, measurable, achievable, relevant, and time-bound) goal-setting concepts and learn how to create goals that are challenging but doable.

Setting goals, however, is a process of self-discovery and a way to match our activities with our highest hopes and beliefs. It's more than just a useful exercise. We face the anxieties and uncertainties that frequently prevent us from achieving our goals as we develop our vision for the future. Through this process, we learn to overcome self-doubt and accept the obstacles that lie ahead.

Setting goals helps us develop the self-control and fortitude needed to overcome hardships because we recognize that each challenge we face presents an opportunity for development and progress. Equipped with lucidity and resoluteness, we go on our journey towards realizing our aspirations, self-assured that we can surmount any obstacles encountered on the road.

Overcoming Difficulties

On our path to achievement, we will unavoidably run into roadblocks and difficulties that could impede our advancement and erode our self-assurance. This chapter looks at methods and approaches to help us deal with the inevitable obstacles that come our way while pursuing our goals.

Through a series of case studies and real-world situations, we explore the typical barriers to success, such as fear of failing and a lack of resources or support. We study the psychology of resilience, discovering how to develop the kind of thinking and attitudes that help people endure hardship and come out stronger and more resilient than they were before.

Overcoming problems, however, requires more than just willpower or resolve; it is a process of self-discovery and accepting the inevitable difficulties and uncertainties that come with pursuing our goals. We learn to use our inner resources to overcome even the most frightening tasks as we face the challenges that lie ahead of us and uncover secret reserves of courage and power within ourselves.

Through the furnace of hardship, we carve out a way ahead, driven by the unwavering conviction that no challenge is insurmountable and no setback is irreversible. We continue forward, resilience serving as our shield and resolve as our sword, understanding that every obstacle we face presents an opportunity for development and advancement.

Closing: Creating the Route for Achievement

We have gained a great sense of purpose and clarity as we come to the end of our investigation into the components of success. This will serve as our road map for the future. We have laid the groundwork for our dreams—a strong foundation of tenacity and resolve that will stand the test of time—from the clarity of our objectives to the resiliency of our spirit.

Equipped with lucidity and resolve, we are positioned on the cusp of opportunity, prepared to set off on an unparalleled voyage of introspection and metamorphosis. We started off into the unknown, sure that we could negotiate the bends and turns of the way ahead, with our aims serving as our guide and our resilience acting as our protection.

Even though the journey may be drawn out and full of difficulties, we find comfort in the idea that each hurdle we face presents a chance for development and advancement. Because it is through pursuing our ambitions that we find the true meaning of humanity and unlock the limitless potential that everyone of us possesses.

Chapter 5: Fostering Innovation: Unlocking the Potential of Imagination

The imagination is a compass and a canvas in the limitless world of creativity; it leads us down unknown paths and motivates us to realize our most audacious ideas. In this section, we explore methods and approaches to foster our imagination and capture the elusive spark of inspiration as we dive into the art and science of creative cultivation.

Imagination Nurturing

The infinite void of the imagination, where the limitations of reality vanish and the only things limiting our options are our own thoughts, is the source of all creative endeavors. This chapter takes us on a journey to develop our imagination and reveal the hidden reservoirs of creativity that are all inside of us. By using a sequence of facilitated activities and contemplative questions, we explore the boundless capacity of our thoughts to conceive of novel worlds, concepts, and opportunities.

By adhering to the tenets of divergent thinking, we can liberate ourselves from the constraints of conventional wisdom and venture into the enormous realm of possibilities that await us. However, encouraging imagination is a path of self-discovery and a way to re-establish a connection with the sense of wonder and curiosity that is fundamental to our humanity. It is more than just a useful activity.

We face the anxieties and worries that frequently prevent us from expressing our creativity as we delve into our imaginations, learning to accept vulnerability and uncertainty as drivers of development and self-expression. We develop the bravery and resiliency required to follow our most audacious ideas and realize our boldest goals in the furnace of our imagination. Equipped with inquisitiveness and inventiveness, we embarked on an expedition of investigation and learning, self-assured in our capacity to utilize our imaginations to alter the surroundings.

Using Your Inspiration

Moments of inspiration, or flashes of insight and intuition that light the way ahead and fan the flames of creation within us, are inevitable when we set out on our creative journeys. This chapter delves into methods and approaches for capturing the elusive spark of inspiration and converting transient epiphanies into durable artistic and innovative creations.

Through a series of case studies and real-life instances, we explore the inspiration that is all around us, ranging from the natural world to the depths of the human experience. We delve into the psychology of creativity, teaching you how to develop the kind of thinking and dispositions that will enable you to spot and grab inspiration when it strikes. However, finding inspiration is a journey of mindfulness—a process of developing awareness and receptivity to the world around us—rather than merely being the result of luck or chance. As we learn to appreciate the beauties of the world, we find that inspiration can come from the most unlikely sources, such as the profound wisdom of a stranger's remarks or the fleeting beauty of a sunset.

We discover how to trust our gut feelings and welcome the creative process with open minds and hearts amid the furnace of inspiration. Equipped with inquisitiveness and openness, we embarked upon an expedition of investigation and revelation, confident in our capacity to elevate the commonplace to the remarkable via the influence of inspiration.

Final Thoughts: Accepting the Creative Process

We are filled with a deep sense of amazement and wonder at the limitless potential that each of us possesses as we come to the end of our investigation into developing creativity. We have set out on a unique self-discovery adventure that has led us from the depths of our imagination to the pinnacles of our creativity. This trip has lit the way to self-expression and fulfillment. Equipped with inquisitiveness and inventiveness, we find ourselves on the cusp of opportunity, prepared to unleash the full force of our imagination and utilize the inspiration of others to revolutionize the world in which we live. We ventured into the unknown with imagination serving as our guide and courage as our compass, sure that we could go ahead and create a future rich with possibility, beauty, and innovation.

And even if the journey may be drawn out and difficult, we find comfort in the idea that each barrier we face presents a chance for development and self-discovery. We uncover the genuine nature of humanity and the limitless potential that each of us possesses when we follow our creative vision.

Chapter 6: Creating Your Route: Managing the Path to Success

The road to success in pursuing our goals is rarely straight. It's a narrow route with lots of opportunities and difficulties along the way. This part covers the key techniques for creating and navigating our route to our objectives, from careful planning to flexible adjustment when circumstances change.

Organizing and carrying out

A meticulously designed plan is the foundation of each successful undertaking; it is a road map that shows us the way to our intended goal. This chapter delves into the fundamentals of efficient planning and execution, teaching us how to convert our goals into concrete tasks and benchmarks. Through a series of guided exercises and useful tools, we learn to break down our goals into doable activities and prioritize them based on urgency and importance. In order to make the most use of the resources we have, we investigate time management and resource allocation strategies.

Planning, however, is a process of self-discovery—a way to match our activities with our highest goals and values—rather than only being a matter of practicalities. We face the anxieties and uncertainties that frequently prevent us from achieving our goals as we develop our vision for the future. Through this process, we learn to overcome self-doubt and accept the obstacles that lie ahead. Through the rigorous process of preparation and implementation, we develop the self-control and fortitude required to endure hardships, understanding that each challenge presents a chance for development and advancement.

Equipped with lucidity and resoluteness, we go on our journey towards realizing our aspirations, self-assured that we can surmount any obstacles encountered on the road.

Getting Used to Change

We all face unforeseen detours, obstacles, and setbacks on our path to achieving our goals, which have the potential to stop us in our tracks. In this chapter, we'll look at methods and approaches for adjusting to change and developing the resilience and grace necessary to deal with the constantly changing circumstances in our lives. Through a series of case studies and real-life situations, we explore the common sources of change and uncertainty that occur in our personal and professional lives. We delve into the psychology of resilience, discovering how to develop the kind of thinking and attitudes that allow change to be accepted as an inherent and necessary aspect of life.

However, adjusting to change requires more than just perseverance; it's also a process of self-discovery, where one must learn to embrace the unknown and develop the adaptability and flexibility required to endure in a constantly shifting world. We find secret reserves of bravery and power within ourselves as we face the unknowns ahead, and we learn to use these inner resources to overcome even the most difficult obstacles.

We learn to trust our instincts and welcome the creative possibilities of uncertainty in the furnace of change, understanding that every challenge we face presents a chance for personal development and revelation. Equipped with adaptation and resilience, we embarked on an expedition of exploration and learning, sure of our capacity to handle the detours and turns in front of us.

Closing: Creating Your Own Route to Achievement

We are left with a strong sense of purpose and clarity as we wrap up our investigation of creating our road map for success. This will serve as our road map going forward. We have laid the groundwork for our dreams, a strong foundation of perseverance and fortitude that will endure the test of time, from the careful preparation of our objectives to the quick adaptation to change.

Equipped with lucidity and resoluteness, we are positioned on the cusp of potential, prepared to seize the upcoming obstacles and prospects. We ventured into the unknown, trusting that we could negotiate the curves and turn on the way to realizing our aspirations, with flexibility serving as our blade and resilience as our shield.

And even if the journey may be drawn out and difficult, we find comfort in the idea that each barrier we face presents a chance for development and self-discovery. Because it is through pursuing our ambitions that we find the true meaning of humanity and unlock the limitless potential that everyone of us possesses.

Chapter 7: The Value of Persistence:

Maintaining Motion Despite Obstacles

Persistence is not just a virtue but also a need when it comes to pursuing our dreams; it is the ability to stay true to our objectives and aspirations in the face of difficulty and disappointment. This section explores the fundamental elements of persistence, covering topics such as developing resilience in the face of setbacks and learning important lessons from them.

The ability to bounce back from setbacks

The path to success will inevitably include failure, which serves as a test of our tenacity and commitment. This chapter examines the value of resilience in the face of adversity and teaches readers how to overcome setbacks with poise and resolve. Through a series of case studies and real-world situations, we explore the typical causes of failure that emerge in both our personal and professional lives. We delve into the psychology of resilience, discovering how to develop the kind of thinking and attitudes that allow us to accept failure as an inherent and necessary aspect of life. However, resilience is a voyage of self-discovery—a process of accepting vulnerability and uncertainty as catalysts for growth and self-improvement—rather than merely a question of willpower or drive. We learn to access our inner resources to overcome even the most difficult obstacles when we face the failures that lie ahead and uncover secret reserves of courage and strength within ourselves.

Failure serves as a crucible where we learn to trust our gut feelings and welcome the creative possibilities of uncertainty, understanding that every obstacle we face presents a chance for personal development. Equipped with fortitude and resoluteness, we embarked upon an expedition of investigation and revelation, self-assured in our capacity to maneuver the winding routes that lay ahead.

Acquiring Knowledge from Failures

Failure presents a priceless opportunity for personal development and advancement—a chance to draw insightful conclusions from failures and utilize them in our future endeavors. This chapter examines methods and approaches for growing from failures and using them as a springboard for personal development.

We investigate the underlying causes of our failures, finding patterns and habits that may have contributed to our setbacks through a series of guided exercises and reflective prompts. We study the concepts of introspection and reflection, learning how to face our errors with bravery and humility. However, learning from failures is a process of self-discovery—embracing the lessons that failure has to offer and putting them to use in our future endeavors—rather than merely analyzing

them. We learn to accept failure as a teacher rather than a foe when we face the impending failures and uncover secret reserves of knowledge and insight within ourselves.
We develop a growth mindset—a resilient, inquisitive attitude that enables us to see failure as a chance for personal development—in the furnace of adversity. Equipped with modesty and resoluteness, we embarked upon an expedition of introspection and learning, confident in our capacity to maneuver the detours leading to our aspirations.

Conclusion: Maintaining Energy Despite Obstacles

We have gained a great sense of purpose and clarity as we come to the end of our examination of the value of perseverance. This will serve as our road map for the future. We have created a strong foundation of perseverance and fortitude that will endure the test of time, one that will support our dreams, from our ability to bounce back from failure to our ability to learn from mistakes.

Equipped with tenacity and resolve, we are prepared to seize the chances and obstacles that lie ahead as we stand on the cusp of possibility. We ventured into the unknown, trusting that we could find our way through the many turns leading to our goals, with curiosity serving as our compass and humility as our guide.

Even if the journey may be drawn out and difficult, we find comfort in the idea that each obstacle we face presents a chance for personal development and exploration. Because it is through pursuing our ambitions that we find the true meaning of humanity and unlock the limitless potential that everyone of us possesses.

Chapter 8: Networking and Cooperation: Building Connections for Success

In today's ever-changing world of personal and professional development, networking and teamwork are crucial cornerstones that help us succeed. This section explores the importance of establishing robust support networks and utilizing connections to accomplish our objectives.

Constructing support systems

A network of people who support, mentor, and assist along the road is the foundation of any successful undertaking. This chapter delves into the significance of building strong support networks that foster our goals and assist us in overcoming obstacles along the way.

Through a series of case studies and real-life situations, we explore the different shapes that support systems can take, from friends and family to mentors and advisers. We explore the psychology of social support and how supportive relationships might help us be more resilient and motivated when faced with challenges.

However, creating support networks involves more than just surrounding oneself with positive people; it's a reciprocal process that involves providing and receiving help in equal measure. We learn to help and encourage others by developing deep ties with them, which fosters a mutually beneficial ecosystem of cooperation and support.

We learn the value of belonging and community—the sense of solidarity that comes from realizing we are not traveling alone—in the furnace of creating support networks. Equipped with the fortitude and inspiration of our social circle, we embarked on our journey with revitalized self-assurance and resoluteness, prepared to tackle any obstacles that may arise.

Making use of connections

Success in today's interconnected world frequently depends on our capacity to establish and capitalize on deep connections with others. This chapter looks at methods for growing our network and using relationships to further our objectives and ambitions. Using a number of useful hints and methods, we discover how to build a network of contacts across many fields and sectors.

We examine the fundamentals of networking, from going to gatherings and conferences to using the internet and social media to broaden our reach. However, networking is a process of creating real connections based on mutual respect, trust, and common interests rather than just gathering business cards or LinkedIn contacts. We develop our ability to listen intently, provide value, and look for chances for cooperation and partnership as we interact with people in our industry.

Through networking, we learn about the transforming power of connection and how to take advantage of the possibilities, resources, and collective wisdom that exist within our social circles. Equipped with a varied array of connections and associates, we embark with renewed self-assurance and zeal, cognizant of the copious resources and prospects at our disposal.

In summary, creating paths together

As we come to the end of our investigation into networking and collaboration, we are reminded of the enormous influence that relationships may have on our path to success. Our development and effect can be amplified and accelerated by fostering meaningful relationships, as evidenced by the depth and quality of our support networks. Equipped with this understanding, we ventured out into the world with a revitalized sense of mission and resolve, prepared to create connections, establish bridges, and work together with others to realize our ambitions. Because it is through cooperation and teamwork that we uncover the full potential of people and open up the boundless opportunities that each of us possesses.

Chapter 9: Managing Uncertainty and Taking Risks to Reach Your Goals

Being open to danger and uncertainty in the dynamic field of professional and personal development is frequently the spark that ignites revolutionary change. This section explores the fine line that separates taking measured risks from throwing caution to the wind and offers methods for overcoming uncertainty and fear along the way.

Analyzed risks as opposed to blind bets

Although there is always some risk involved in advancement, not all hazards are the same. This chapter examines the differences between blind gambles, or careless acts motivated by impulse or desperation, and calculated risks, or purposeful judgments guided by thorough thought and foresight.

We investigate the possible benefits and drawbacks of both

ways of taking risks through a number of case studies and real-world scenarios. We examine the emotional and cognitive biases that might affect how we perceive risk as we delve into the psychology of decision-making. However, taking calculated risks is a mindset—a readiness to embrace uncertainty and step outside our comfort zone in pursuit of our goals—rather than only a matter of analysis. We learn to follow our instincts and exercise caution when faced with uncertainty because we are aware that every chance we take presents an opportunity for development.

We learn the transforming power of moving outside our comfort zone and embracing the difficulties that lie ahead in the furnace of taking risks. Equipped with fortitude and tenacity, we embarked upon an expedition of investigation and learning, sure of our capacity to confront the unpredictabilities that awaited us.

Handling doubt and fear

Although fear and doubt are common companions on the path

to development and success, they don't have to be roadblocks. This chapter delves into techniques for controlling these intense feelings and using them to propel us forward. Through a variety of useful hints and methods, we learn to recognize the root causes of fear and doubt and create plans for facing and conquering them. We study the concepts of mindfulness and self-compassion, learning how to develop a resilient and self-assured mindset in the face of difficulty.

However, controlling fear and uncertainty requires more than simply willpower; it is a process of self-discovery, facing our deepest anxieties and insecurities, and learning to accept them as natural parts of being human. We find secret reserves of bravery and strength within ourselves as we face the challenges ahead, and we learn to use these inner resources to get past even the most difficult situations.

We develop perspective and resilience in the furnace of

uncertainty and anxiety because we understand that every obstacle we face presents a chance for personal development. Equipped with bravery and tenacity, we embarked upon an expedition of exploration and revelation, sure of our capacity to successfully negotiate the uncharted territory up front.

Final Thoughts: Accepting the Journey

We have gained a deep sense of purpose and clarity as we come to the end of our investigation into accepting risk and uncertainty. This will serve as our road map for the future. We have created a strong foundation of resiliency and perseverance that will endure the test of time, one that will support our aspirations, starting with the measured risks we take and ending with the anxieties we face. Equipped with this understanding, we venture forth into the world with a revitalized sense of mission and resolve, prepared to seize the chances and challenges that await us. Because it is in the spirit of risk-taking and uncertainty that we uncover the true nature of humanity and unlock the limitless potential that each of us possesses.

Chapter 10: Maintaining the Flames: Maintaining Momentum

Maintaining momentum on the path to our objectives and dreams is frequently essential to long-term success. This section looks at methods for maintaining motivation and acknowledging progress along the route.

Maintaining Motivation

Sustaining motivation is crucial to keeping up our momentum as we work towards our goals. This chapter delves into the psychology of motivation and examines useful strategies for maintaining inspiration and goal focus. Through a series of case studies and real-world situations, we study how various elements, including intrinsic rewards and external incentives, affect motivation. We examine the fundamentals of self-control and goal-setting while learning to develop routines and habits that aid in our advancement. However, maintaining motivation requires more than simply willpower; it is a process of self-discovery and bringing our behaviors into line with our highest goals and values. By understanding the motivation behind our objectives, we can draw from a reservoir of zeal and inspiration that keeps us moving forward in the face of difficulty. Through the trial by fire of motivation, we develop a growth mindset—a resilient, inquisitive attitude that enables us to surmount setbacks and keep going for our goals. Equipped with resolute determination and a clear objective, we embarked on a voyage of exploration and revelation, sure of our capacity to maintain our pace and accomplish our objectives.

Honoring Significant Occasions It's critical that we take the time to recognize and celebrate our victories as we go forward on our path to success.

This chapter examines the value of commemorating accomplishments and useful strategies for indicating our development.

Through a sequence of guided activities and thought-provoking questions, we develop the ability to acknowledge the value of all of our achievements, no matter how minor. We investigate the psychology of celebration, discovering how encouragement can keep us moving forward and increase our motivation.

However, commemorating achievements is more than just a formality—it's a potent means of fostering resilience and self-assurance. We build a sense of pride and success when we take time to recognize our accomplishments, which fortifies our determination and encourages us to keep moving forward.

In the furnace of celebration, we find the happiness and contentment that come from appreciating our accomplishments and paying tribute to the effort and commitment that got us there. Equipped with thankfulness and admiration, we embarked on our journey with fresh vigor and eagerness, prepared to take on the obstacles that lie ahead.

In conclusion: Continuing the Trip

We are reminded of the value of maintaining motivation and acknowledging accomplishments along the path as we draw to a close our investigation of maintaining momentum. From the peaks of inspiration to the victories of accomplishment, we have examined the crucial components that propel our development and maintain us on our path to success.

Equipped with this understanding, we venture forth into the world with a revitalized sense of mission and resolve, prepared to take on any obstacles that may arise. Because it is in the spirit of celebration and tenacity that we find the real joy and fulfillment of pursuing our dreams and ambitions.

Chapter 11: Realizing Your Dreams: An Introspective and Generous Path

To achieve our goals, we must develop an attitude of generosity and thankfulness. This section examines the value of giving back to others and the transformational power of introspection and thankfulness.

Gratitude and Introspection

To travel toward our dreams with respect and intention, reflection and thankfulness are necessary disciplines. This chapter delves into the importance of setting aside time to evaluate our achievements and show thankfulness for all the benefits in our lives. We develop the habit of mindfulness and reflection through a series of guided exercises and contemplative questions.

We study the concepts of thankfulness, discovering how to be appreciative of the wealth all around us, and taking delight in the small things in life. However, thankfulness and introspection are more than simply lofty ideals; they are life-changing activities that have the capacity to raise our consciousness and alter our viewpoint.

We develop a feeling of serenity and happiness that propels our advancement and carries us through difficulties when we take time to consider our path and give thanks for the gifts we've experienced.

We learn about the significant effects that these practices can have on our contentment and well-being in the furnace of introspection and thankfulness. Equipped with an enhanced appreciation for the voyage, we embarked upon it with revitalized vigor and excitement, prepared to seize the chances and obstacles that awaited us.

Putting Something Back

It's critical to keep in mind the value of giving back and having a positive influence on other people's lives as we work to achieve our own goals. This chapter delves into the idea of paying it forward as well as the transformational potential of compassion and generosity. We explore the cascading effects of kindness and generosity—from tiny acts of service to larger-scale philanthropic endeavors—through a series of case studies and real-life examples. We study the concepts of empathy and altruism, learning how to develop a giving spirit that benefits people around us as well as ourselves.

However, giving back is not merely a moral duty; it's also a significant chance for personal development and fulfillment. Giving of ourselves to others allows us to feel the happiness and fulfillment that come from changing the world for the better. We learn that serving others and the greater good brings us true fulfillment instead of pursuing our personal goals.

The test of paying it forward reveals the transformational potential of kindness and compassion. Equipped with an attitude of service and an overflowing heart of appreciation, we embarked on a path of influence and effect, prepared to improve the lives of people around us and leave a lasting legacy of compassion and generosity.

Conclusion: Accepting the Journey

We are reminded of the value of introspection, thankfulness, and giving as we come to the end of our investigation into realizing our aspirations. Our journey has been enriched by our exploration of the fundamental components that give our lives meaning and fulfillment, ranging from the depths of reflection to the pinnacles of service. Equipped with this understanding, we venture forth into the world with a revitalized sense of mission and resolve, prepared to seize the chances and challenges that await us. We find the real delight and fulfillment of pursuing our goals and objectives when we approach the trip with an attitude of contemplation, thankfulness, and giving.

In conclusion, the journey continues.

After finishing our investigation into the complexities of realizing our aspirations, we find ourselves at a crossroads, where we can reflect and look forward to starting the next phase of our adventure. In this concluding section, we consider the lessons discovered, the obstacles surmounted, and the future course of action.

Considering the trip

Perseverance, resilience, and progress have all been weaved into the tapestry of our journey towards realizing our dreams. Through it all, we have persevered in pursuing our goals despite experiencing both triumphant and defeating moments along the way. We acknowledge the challenges we've encountered and the lessons we've gained as we look back on the journey. We honor the triumphs—large and small—that have propelled our development and molded our personalities. And we give thanks to everyone who has accompanied us on this journey with their encouragement and support.

However, we also realize that our search for contentment is far from over as we take a moment to consider the trip thus far. The road never stops, calling us onward with fresh obstacles to overcome, new heights to scale, and fresh aspirations to follow.

Accepting Evolution and Growth

We accept that growth and evolution are inevitable as we look to the future. The path to achieving our goals is a dynamic one that requires constant learning and adaptation rather than a set course. We understand that success is a journey rather than a destination, one that is shaped by our ability to adapt and welcome change. By accepting change and progress, we make a commitment to lifelong learning and personal development. We understand that pursuing our goals necessitates going outside of our comfort zones, facing our anxieties and concerns, and facing the unknown with bravery and resiliency.

However, we also take solace in the understanding that development and evolution are collaborative processes. Knowing that we are not traveling alone gives us strength in the community's encouragement and support. Joining forces with our common goals and humanity, we set out on a journey of growth and self-discovery.

Considering the Future

We are excited and full of expectation as we stand on the precipice of the future. There are countless options on the road ahead, each of which could be a step closer to our goals and desires. However, we look to the future with humility and thankfulness, aware of the difficulties and unknowns that lie ahead. We understand that pursuing our aspirations is not without its challenges, but we rise to the occasion with bravery

and a resolute mindset, knowing that every hurdle we clear progresses us towards our goals by one step.
Therefore, as we continue on our path, we do so with optimism and hope, propelled by our ambitions for the future and the lessons learned from the past. Knowing that the journey itself is the best reward, we get closer to realizing our dreams with every step we take.
In conclusion, achieving our goals is a common search for development, resiliency, and self-discovery rather than a solo one. Let's embrace the obstacles, rejoice in the successes, and keep pushing for excellence in everything we do as we set out on our adventure. Because the voyage is still ongoing and it holds out the prospect of a better tomorrow,

www.ingramcontent.com/pod-product-compliance
Lightning Source LLC
Chambersburg PA
CBHW070417230526
45471CB00006B/2849